BOOK BENCHERS
PUBLICATIONS
PRESENTS

YOUNG FELLOWS

Compiled by

Sanjay Naik

Ayush Mondal

AELAY PUBLICATION

A dream come true for every writers out there. We spot every possible problem for the writers, help in rectifying them and guide them towards the best outcome. We make sure to understand your needs, dreams and expectations, and nourish them with our services and stop not until we fulfill your dreams. The writers have a right and freedom to choose what they want here. They have us to guide them through the hardest path untill the end. Believe in us.

Aelay Publication - by a writer for the writers.

BOOK BENCHERS

Book Benchers is the affiliate of Aelay publication. Both the publication is handled by Astro.
Aelay plays the role of publishing solo books.
And Book Benchers is epically for publishing anthologies.

Book Benchers have 2 different teams.

1. Tamil
2. English/Hindi

Never mind what our main motive is to help all the budding writers, who are seeking for their dream of publishing their own book to come true.

We are there to help out everyone.
In guiding for starting up with your carrier in compiling until finishing up your full book.

COPYRIGHT

(Affiliate by Aelay Publish)

Copyright © Sanjay Naik& Ayush Mondal 2021
All rights are reserved. No part of this publication may be reproduced, stored in a retrieval system or transmitted in any form or by any means , electronic , mechanical, photocopying, recording or otherwise, without the prior written permission of the consent of it's writer. The opinions/ contents expressed in this book are solely of the author and do not represent the opinions/ standings/ thoughts of publisher.

Design And Executed by

ISBN : 978-93-91423-77-3
Page : 118

Acknowledgement

Acknowledgement is essential to boost up passion, making person more valid and precious, giving the team a great progress that makes worth.

We would like to use this opportunity to thank each and everyone who all the people involved in this book and, more specifically, to all the co - authors .Without your support, this book would not have become a reality.

We would like to thank each one of the authors for their contributions. Our sincere gratitude to all who contributed their time and expertise to this book.

We wish to acknowledge the valuable contributions of the Publication regarding the improvement of quality, coherence, and content. Last but not least, we would like to extend our gratitude to parents and friends who have been a huge support through the book.

FOUNDER

IRUDAGA ASTRO

Irudaga Astro, From Tirunelveli, Founder of
Aelay and BB (Book Benchers)
He had completed his BE.
He has written 3 Tamil poetry book's which
hits the top list on social media!
His main aim is to allow the writers to
publish their words as their book rather than
just Posting them on Insta.

LINK AND POSTER MAKER

CATHERINE ASMI T

Catherine Asmi T, From Tirunelveli
She has completed her M.com
Her passion is Drawing and Designing.

TEAM HEAD

She is a passionate writer from Chennai. Writing makes her pressure go away. She had played the role of co-author for more than 100+ Antho's. She would like to thank her parents and her Loveable Brother for supporting her rather than stopping her from what she wanted to do! For being the main reason for achieving her dreams. As well as for standing beside her in all the ups and downs. Whenever she feels like she needs to get out of her stressful timing or feels like she needs peacefulness, she starts to paint, she would never mind sitting in the same place for so many hours when it comes to her painting. She believes that anyone could hurt her, But never her books could!!

Catch her in Insta and FB
Insta: @theinnocentheart
FB: KA. PARINASRI

Index

23. S. Suganthi
24. Ankita Mishra
25. Sonal Prajapati
26. Srija Sadhukhan
27. Ravishanker Nishad (ARVI)
28. Priya Singh
29. Ishita Saxena
30. Akkshaya prasanna
31. Dakshita Jaiswal
32. Ankur Mishra
33. Prakash Turiya (Raghuwanshi)
34. Prakhar Raghuwanshi
35. Bhawna Mehta
36. Mansi Solanki
37. Naveen Bhardwaj
38. Anusha Sathia
39. N. Krishnaveni
40. Deesha Soni
41. Yogesh Gurjar Chinu
42. Poetry Khakholia
43. Kajal Bhargav
44. Anamika
45. Ms. Ishrat Jahan Noormohammed Khan
46. Sravani Kommayya
47. Mihir Pathak
48. Yuvasri Yelleti
49. Neeraj J
50. Smita G Naidu
51. MS. Chandrika.J.N
52. Jasmine Panda

SANJAY NAIK

Sanjay Naik is from Kharagpur State of West Bengal. He is an Economics graduate (Hons), a writer from the heart and passionate about singing. Through the platform of anthology, he wants to spread love & positivity among his readers and wants to heal his readers' hearts with his magical words. Sanjay is at utmost peace when he pens his emotions. He believes that the power of his words, will heal the wounds of many readers. Till now participated in 200+ Anthologies as a CO-AUTHOR. He is Compiler of anthology "SELF HAPPINESS" , "SCREAM" & " SARANG". And now compiled more than 50 + Anthologies.
Instagram:- @the_poetry_wo

ENLIGHTENMENT IN YOUR WORDS

I have a deep connection with words
Which thrives in my mind inside only
The mind is eager to know
The meaning of every word
This is my means of fulfillment
It has explained to me the definition of life has
never even made me feel alone whenever the mind
feels heavy
Take a pen and write two words
It seems like I am blessed
To have enlightenment
It makes me happy to be
so tied between words
Where my words are unable
To say anything, by writing
A few words my pen can feel peace

2. AYUSH MONDAL

AYUSH MONDAL, He is studying in B.Com Honors from BRSNC Collage, Barrakpore. He lives in Kolkata, West Bengal (North 24 pgs). He gain more experience through the journey of writing and he wants to learn more. He writes many Poems and Quotes and Short Stories and he is still writing to improve his skills more. Currently, he is working in many different Anthologies about different topics and he is grateful to be a part of this Anthology. He participated in many anthologies as a co-author and he write many Poems and Stories. Now he is working as a compiler but still he is focusing in his writing. He has a passion to write everything. He always says, "Age is just a number, it can never judge you what you can write." He writes all his poems in both Hindi and English language that his poems touch the heart of the readers.

Follow him on: Instagram - ayuman2002

Facebook - Ayush Mondal

MORNING'S GLORY

Today, I woke up in the early morning
Due to lots of work pressure, I fall in asleep
That was so busy day for me, yesterday
I hear the sound of nature, the next morning
Because of, birds are chirping outside
Whistling in it's sweet voice, very low
It broke my drowsiness and tiredness
I walked to the balcony to feel the nature
I breathed heavily the smell of flowers
The fregarant of it, make me very pleased
The cold wind touches my whole face
And blowing from all around and directions
The sun is shinning so far away from me
But it's rays are falling from the high hills
And cover my whole body, face and arms
As it is removing all that negativity and
Spreading only positivity in the vast world
Which makes me very energetic to do
All the works with great enthusiasm.

1. LIPSA DABHI

She is Lipsa Dabhi. She is Author and also good Co-Author. She is eighteen years old; she is student of the computer engineering. She is extraordinary person. She is always good leader. Her mam mrunal prajapati is her inspiration person and also her motivater, her friend Chetna raval also supported to her and her mom Manisha Ben and her father Nilesh Bhai also supported to her for any type of her creativity. She also wrote poems, short stories, shayaries. Her writing skills almost very well and her creative collections are always best.

SMILE

Smile is powerful tool of life,
Smile is unique and creative tool,
Smile is very precious forever,
Smile it's free therapy,
Peace begins with a smile.
Smile at strangers and you just might change a life,
Life is powerful but life with smile is very perfect,
Smile is extra beauty of life,
Smile is creative tool of life,
Smile is important so keep smiling.
Smile it increases your face value,
Smile more smiling can make you and others
happy,
Smile is the key of happy and good life, with smile
life is great,
Smile is always best medicine for all diseases.

2. APOORBA CHATURVEDI

This is Apoorba Chaturvedi from the queen of hills Darjeeling. She enjoys moonlight strolls on the beaches. Just kidding! She is not a fan of any of those things. More seriously, her friends and family would describe her as easy going, a good listener, a wordplay ninja, and the best cappuccino maker in the world.

THERE WAS SOMETHING

There was something in those eyes,
When you glanced at me and grinned,
It seemed to me like life just stopped,
I believe it was not a sin,
To think about you every day long,
And to accompany you in my dreams,
To feel your sleeves around me,
Guarding me it seemed,
When you stretched out and grasped my hand,
Or while your arm was around me,
There was nowhere I would preferably be,
Then right there with you alongside me.

3. MADHUMITHA

A girl of teen and a creative dreamer letting her beautiful thoughts out through pen and paper.

MEMORIES OF LOVE

The most memorable love of my life is my parents
love.
Nothing can be compared to parents love;
The love of standing together walking together
Becoming a proud son of my parents are the
memories of love.
Memories of love doesn't mean spending time with
the loved ones,
memories of love doesn't mean spending time with
your friends
it is all about spending good time with your parents.
Memories of love is about dad scolding you
for not getting good marks in your examination.
Memories of love reminds me of my mom
Taught me reading, writing, handwriting.
The memories of love of my parents will always be
evergreen and cheerful memories.

4. HAR DEEPANSH BAHADUR SINHA

He is Har Deepansh Bahadur Sinha. He belongs to Lucknow, UP. He is a research scholar of Oceanography and has done masters in Geography from National Post Graduate College. Completed his schooling from Study Hall. His hobbies are art, listening to music, cooking & loads of driving. His interest areas are Astronomy, Writing, and Photography & Travelling a lot.

LET'S ACCEPT & RESPECT

When you look at them so suspiciously
It means you are harming them purposely,
They have also got similar rights
For that you must improve your sight.
What happens if they are transgenders
From our acts they feel like strangers,
The more they work for societies betterment
More than that we hurt their sentiments.
What we do is complete partiality
What they suffer is deep inequality,
We just don't want to accept this clarity
That they have got a unique identity.
Already they have been through numerous pain
Our criticism to them is the biggest stain,
What they need from us is encouragement
Together as a family let's attain development.
Towards them pour some humanity
From this day stop this cruelty.

5. TASNEEM SHEIKH

Tasneem Sheikh of Assam, author of '**Tulips Coffee and You**', is a 17 year old poet and writer, co-author of 120+ anthologies and numerous magazines. She was recognized as a young achiever in English Literature by esteemed personalities of Maria's Montessori in 2016. A critic, counsellor and humanitarian, apart from her endearment for literature, she also holds a passion towards music, expressive artwork, creativity and adventures.
Instagram: la_nuit_portrait

THE DAWN

It was in the dawn that everything took place

We were almost singing songs and dancing to the
vintage rhythm,
We were almost laughing and eating our favourite
snacks
Busy with our stories, counting stars on our heads.
All in the dawn, taking a trip to the nearby green
hill
It felt like there was no tomorrow,
We were more alive than the chirping birds.
We went to the city fair while returning back home
We thought the dawns were the best,
Of all times and of all seasons.
The night's almost sleepless and day's lazy,
We were enjoying our time and almost fell in love.
You left and I'm almost alive now.

6. SHIVAM MAURYA

This is Shivam Maurya from Gorakhpur Uttar
Pradesh. He is a writer at heart and passionate about
singing. He wants to spread love and positivity
among his readers and heals his readers' hearts with
his magic words. Shivam is the most peaceful. The
power of his words, he believes, will heal the
wounds of many readers.

दस्तूर

जब-जब दर्द का बादल छाया,
जब ग़म का साया लहराया
जब आंसू पलकों तक आया
जब यह तन्हा दिल घबराया
हमने दिल को यह समझाया,
दिल आखिर तू क्यों रोता है
दुनियां में यूं ही होता है,
यह जो गहरे सन्नाटे हैं
बक्त ने सब को ही बांटे हैं ।
थोड़ा गम है सबका किस्सा थोड़ी धूप है
सबका हिस्सा आंखें तेरी बेकार ही नम हैं,
हर पल एक नया मौसम है क्यों तू ऐसा पल खोता है ।
दिल आखिर तू क्यों रोता है
दुनियां में यूं ही होता है ।।

7. HARSHITA VERMA

Co-author Harshita Verma is a writer from Lucknow. She has completed her graduation in commerce stream. She has been writing poetry for the last few years as her passion. She wants to be a novelist in future.

TIME CHANGES

The time of change
The era of ninties
Revolutions coming in life
The period of differences.
The movies coming in life
The entry of new products
The globalization beginning
Accepting the changes.
The change from telephone
To the new colour television
Everything new coming in
The lively changes of life
When games were played outside
When nature seemed beautiful
The time of pleasure and fun
Gone but will always be remembered.

8. MOHAMMED NIYAZ

Mohammed Niyaz hails from Mumbai - The City of Dreams. He often loves to write poetries and short music video stories for his own youtube channel. Apart from this Mohammed is currently working on his upcoming anthologies, as well writing poetries since 2013. You can find him on facebook/mohammed niyaz as well on instagram @niyazsks.

QUOTE 1

Everyone has unique talent hidden in them.
They just need to make sure they opt it for the
better.
Once they understand the importance of their own.
They can create wonders of what they have.
Never ever dreamt of having through.

QUOTE 2

Life has been an amazing journey.
With ups and downs within the sides.
We may accept or not the truth knows well.
That we cannot stay away from the possibilities.
That can attain us throughout the entire time.

Quote 3

You are the one who can compromise with
everything.
You should reach new heights of it every day.
But not for something's that cause you with.
Lots of pain and efforts for such causes.
That leads you to the path of destruction.

9. ROZY PAUL

Her name is Rozy Paul She belongs to the tea-estate
called Dibrugarh, Assam. She has done M.A.in
journalism. Her hobbies are reading, gardening and
cooking. She likes travelling a lot. Her favourite
quote is 'live and let live'.

ACTIVE MIND: "Young age is the working age with heart and soul so that old age can be kept for rest and roaming with no more tension."

TRUST: "Young people should be trustworthy so can rest of the world keep faith on them."

FRIENDSHIP: "working in a group with team spirit and reach the targeted goal."

10. SONALI MEHER

Hey readers....!! She is Sonali Meher. From - Nuapada, Odisha, India. Currently pursuing for the degree of BAMS at Sri Sri Nursingnath Ayurveda medical College and RI. She is a Doctor by profession and writer by passion. She started writing when a very special moments come in her life and now for her writing is hobby. The writing is the 3rd person in that way of expressing their feelings, emotions and love. Now get a platform to exploring her writing. Hope! You guys like it.

ज़िन्दगी है छोटी-सी

ज़िन्दगी है छोटी-सी
कब कैसे आएगा,जाएगा कुछ पता नहीं
जब तक जीना है, खुशी से सबके साथ जीना है
ज़िन्दगी है छोटी-सी ।।
दुनिया है इतना बड़ा कोई एक हमारे लिए इतना खास हो
जाता है पता भी नहीं चलता
क्यों होता है कैसे होता है पता नहीं
जब तक वो है सब खुश,जब चला जाएगा बोलने को कोई
नहीं होगा,ना ही कोई सुनने को होगा
ज़िन्दगी है छोटी-सी ।।
वो अनजान हो के भी हमारे लिए खास होता है
जब चला जाता है दुनिया वाले तो क्या कुछ भी बोलेंगे,
किन्तु वो हमारे दिलों में ऐसे ही रहता है हमारे पास पास,
दूर होके भी दोनों पास होते है
ज़िन्दगी है छोटी-सी ।।

11. CATHERINE SHEENA

Sheena Catherine is a girl with plenty of dreams.
She is a nineteen years old girl who is still trying to
achieve her dreams. Her pen name is
sheenacathrinebelle. She likes to write poems, short
stories, quotes etc. She is a broad minded person.
She believes that words speak greater than action so
she writes from her heart.

MOM IT'S YOUR DAY

It's your day, Mom,
To celebrate life with your beautiful smile,
As you've successfully completed an another year.
I wish you to Smile always like a radiant Star
shining in my starry nights.
Mom, I'm not your perfect daughter,
I'm not able to give you anything,
But I give you this poem on your special day.
Mom, I failed to become someone you're proud of,
But I promise, One day I'll make you proud.
I wish you a wonderful day with all my Love.
Mom, I don't have job, I don't have money,
I don't have presents to surprise you,
But I have my boundless Love,
And I'll always make you happy Mom.
Wish you many more happy returns of the day,
Dear Mom.

12. NIKITA YADAV

Almost all good writings begin with the terrible efforts. You just need to start from somewhere. Nikita Yadav is an immature writer which is not a writer by profession but only loves to write. She belongs to Haryana, Gurgaon city. She is BSC final year medical science student along with this she loves to share her thoughts an experience through her writings. She respect others feelings and emotions and never hurt anyone's feelings and emotions through her content. She says, "Write the words which comes from depth of your heart not for the money"

I wonder what he had done to me,
I wonder why he had done to me.
My fault had made him anger,
But my sorry is nothing in his under.
Is this was a previous revenge?
Or step towards his change?
My tears, my weeping nothing change his feelings,
I cry, I shout, but there is nothing to speak with
mouth.
The first time when I met him,
Was more than a beautiful dream.
His glittering and wonderful eyes make me more
and more hypnotize.
But now there is everything to scream,
It is bad than a hell dreamed.
I am still wondering what he had done to me,
Why he had done to me?

13. SHASWAT SOURAV SAHOO

Shaswat Sourav Sahoo, is an eighteen-something adventurer who grew up traversing the wonders through the pages of metaphors. He fell in love with books and never reverted. Today he is pursuing his studies and living a clichéd life at NISER as an Integrated M.Sc. research scholar. He has been recently awarded with the Global Achiever's Award. When he is not sorrunded by words you can spot him fancying and pampering the dogs. He is a jovial kind of person revamping his past grief events into allured moments. He loves voicing his emotions and get it penned down. Another feather to his cap is his intense intimacy with taking shots. Nevertheless, he is also impassioned for painting, playing indoors, origami. He is looking forward his life being a polymath and pour on whatever he possesses within and wishes never to quell it.

THE UNFEIGNEDLY NIGHT

It was a gloomy dreadful night.
She was in the middle
And i held her soft hands tight
With exotic obstacles on our left and right.

Beside her stood my friend,
My friend who was with me
In all my odds and give a hand
Since my childhood, I should tend.

The more grew the night,
The more I lost my sight
Betwixt the ghostly road ride,
We made our way upto the height.

Deep down seemed a lamp,
Grumpy and feisty like a camp,
My heart dripped and sank,
Skipped a bit as came the lamp.

The other fingers were intertwined,
Her head rested upon her shoulders.
Love stained and cursive need,
They made themselves a perfect seed.

Unaware and oblivious, they, Hit them hard as
anybody could say. I left her hand and wiped my
tears. After all, It's the end of a Friendship and my
eternal love That nix in the world could ever bear.

14. DOLLY VADHVANI

नमस्कार, इनका नाम डोली वाधवाणी है ! ये आंनद गुजरात से हैं ! इन्होंने गुजरात युनिवर्सिटी गांधीनगर से B.Com और सोमनाथ युनिवर्सिटी से PGDCA किया है ! अभी दो साल से Computer Operator की तरह जोब कर रहीं हैं ! डोली को अपनी भावनाएं लिखना बेहद पसंद है ! इनकी जिंदगी का एक ही असूल है, तुम आज को जियो और आज मे जियो फिर देखो जिंदगी कितनी खूबसूरत है...!

राधा-कृष्ण

कृष्ण जैसे प्रित की आश किसको ना होगी...!
राधा बनने की चाह किसे ना होगी...!
राधा-कृष्ण की कहानी रही अनोखी है...!
इसमें कहीं ना हार ना जीत है...!
कृष्ण ने भले ही कितनी भी गोपियां क्यूं ना बनाई...!
फिर भी राधा ही उसके मन को भाई है...!
कहते हैं ना आसमां में कितने ही तारे क्यूं ना हो...!
पर चांद की कमी किसी से भरपाई ना हुई...!
बस ऐसे ही कुछ कृष्ण के लिए राधा छाई...!
राधा-कृष्ण की जुदाई ने ही उनके प्रेम की कहानी रची...!
राधा ने भी खूब दुख झेले इसलिए तो कृष्ण के नाम के आगे भी
राधा समाई...!

15. VAISHNAWI KUMARI

Vaishnawi kumari is from Patna, Bihar. She is a poetess, co-author and Hindi writer. She is studying as a computer science student in NSIT BIHTA. Her hobbies are dancing, singing and writing. She likes to decorate her feelings on a paper.. She is motivated by her father. She become co-author of 150+ successful anthologies with different publications and 10+ world record Anthologies. And now she is working as a author of 4 Anthologies with different publications. If you want to connect with her personally then follow her Instagram handle @kumarivaishnawi and for her quote and poetry then follow @mystic.vaishu

THE ERA WAS SOMETHING ELSE

We depict the things of that era in such a way,
As we fill small happiness in our bag, that era also
had a different fun...
To love, to express and to wait,
How beautiful would that moment have been....
When people used to express their love with letters,
Letter arriving early and arriving soon,
There was a gathering full of notes...
There was a different style in each work.
There was fragrance and there was a feeling and
knowing it was a different...
Each color had a uniqueness...
There was a feeling in the songs of those days.
There was a touch.....
Know that era is so hidden in today's era Which is
not only difficult but impossible to remove,
Feel that no matter how much we today do not get
the feeling that was in that era,
All these things were taken care of with respect to
the Unity family and today no one even knows the
word of The whole name of brother...
Is there dignity, shame, shame, humility?
In those days it was seen...
And in today's era it is as if people have sold
There is no synergy between that era and today's
era... What a great time it was...

16. PRACHI GUPTA

Prachi Gupta is a Passionate writer who loves to create her imaginary arts in a random canvas. She is pursuing her studies in BBA and lives in Allahabad known as the pure city of Sangam. She loves to sing and watching movies in her free time. She is a shy and a open-minded girl at the same time For more information can follow her and contact:- Prachiguptt0210@gmail.com @prachigupta3435 @prachi_gupta_210

THOSE DAYS

I remember,
My those days
Where I was a girl with sparkling skills

No matter,
Where I go
I was always tend to shine the surroundings

I remember,
My those days
Where I was busy in making my life
Where I had no stress to work or solving these
damn rifes

I remember,
My those days
Where everyone was aware with my Attitude and
Heights

But now,
I became a silent girl with no Delights .

17. KALAMKAAR

मेरा नाम कलमकार हैं! में उत्तराखंड का रहनेवाला हु मगर मेरठ (उत्तरप्रदेश) में रह रहा हु! उसे पड़ना और लिखना पसंद हैं! उसकी रूचि लिखने में बहुत हैं! उन्हें लिखना बहुत प्रिया हैं!मैंने 850 + से ज्यादा anthology में सहलेखक के रूप में काम किया हैं, उनको लेखन मैं 720 +सम्मान पत्र से नवाज़ा गया हैं!उसने 28 फेब्रुअरी 2020 से लिखना शुरू किया था! उसकी 2 एंथोलोग्य Omg Book of record के लिए गयी थी जिसमे से 1 एंथोलोग्य omg book of record प्रपात किया हैं! जिसका वह सेह लेखक है और उस पुस्तक का नाम लपोसया! उनका इंस्टा kalamkaar51 हैं! उसको फल से ज्यादा कर्म पर विशवास हैं!

बुरा ख़्याल ना आने दे

हार जाये अगर ज़िन्दगी में कभी तो खुदको कमज़ोर ना
समझे!
सोचकर खुदको अवसाद में ना जाने दे
ये तो सिर्फ एक पहलु है ज़िन्दगी है!
बुरा ख़्याल ना आने दे!
हार कर फिर जीत मिल सकती है दोबारा!
हार हालातो के आगे खुदको ना मानने दे!
लड़े फिर से और जीते फिर से एक योद्धा की तरह!
और बुरा ख्याल ना आने दे!
ठोकर खाकर ही आदमी कुछ सीखता है!
सकारात्मक सोच रखे और अपने अंदर आने दे!
बुरे ख्यालो आपके ज़ेहन में कभी ना आये!
बुरा ख़्याल ना आने दे!
सबसे खुदको सर्वश्रेष्ठ माने हमेशा से!
कमज़ोर मानकर खुदको किसी से यूँही ना हारने दे!
लड़े जबतक जीत आपकी नहीं हो जाती!
और बुरा ख़्याल ना आने दे!

18. DHARSHINI M.

She is dharshini from kovilpatti. She is pursing masters in English. She has huge interest in writing. She loves to share her thought and emotion through her writing. She has done many anthologies as co author . She has published a book named 'vox of mine '.

LIFE QUOTES

1. Life is bound with temporary stuffs
As we are all are temporary ones here
But we are all running to grab permanent one.

2. The extreme love is quite dangerous
We need to be limited with all
To know our value and our position in their heart.

19. ANKITA NAHAR

Ankita Nahar, physically she live in AJMER, RAJASTHAN but heartly live in everywhere. She is too much passionate about writing. She has always found comfort in words, and that's what attracts everyone. Writing is her therapy, she writes what she feels and experiences in her life. You can take a look at her writings on Instagram @naharankita1

YES I GUESS

Yes I guess
The society we live in
About that
Nothing wrong to say

But now say nothing
Maybe it's too late
Better than rubbing hands
To speak now

I don't like that society

Where it doesn't work
Bribes are given
Where there is no progress
Others are thrown down

Where girls don't go out
Are advised to leave
Where innocent girls
Not seen as safe

Where corruption happens every day
Where rapists roam freely
Yes I don't like
This type of society.

20. KUSHAGRA PATHAK

इनका नाम कुशाग्र पाठक है । ये लखनऊ से है । ये तृतीय वर्ष के छात्र है। ये 20 वर्ष के थे तब से लेखन का कार्य कर रहे है। ये बहुत से लेखको से प्रेरित हे लेकिन सबसे ज्यादा ये कुमार विश्वास जी से प्रेरित है।इनका लिखना शुरू करने का उद्देश्य लोगों कि मदद करना और लोगों को मदद करने के लिए तैयार करना है । ये मुख्य रूप से सामाजिक और विभिन्न लोगों कि मानसिकता के बारे में लिखते है।

भगवान

मेरे लिए मेरे माता-पिता ही मेरे ईश्वर है,
ईश्वर ने खुद उन्हें हमारे लिए चुना है,
जा नहीं सकते वो हर जगह एक ही वक्त पर,
इसलिए उन्होंने माता-पिता को भेजा है,
खुशनसीब हूं मैं जो मेरे जहां को रोशन किया है,
हे ईश्वर तुने मुझ पर बड़ा ही परोपकार किया है....
और जिंदगी में सुख-दुख तो आते ही रहते है,
पर इनसे लड़ने की ताकत भी तो तू देता है,
फिर भी लोग जरा सी परेशानी में तुझे कोसने लग जाते है,
कि ईश्वर तुने मेरे लिए किया ही क्या है,
ये कोरोना काल हमारे पापों का ही नतीजा है,
ना कि ये ईश्वर का रचा है,
विधी का विधान है जिसने गलत किया है उसे उसका दण्ड
मिलना है,
तो क्यों ये भूल हमने ईश्वर को ही कोषा है....
जब भी टूटी मैं तो माता पिता ने मुझे हिम्मत दिया है,
क्योंकि ईश्वर ने उन्हें हमारे लिए ही भेजा है,
हर मुसीबत से मेरे माता-पिता ने मुझे बचाया है,
ईश्वर ने ही उन्हें मेरा ईश्वर बनाया है,
मैं दिल से तेरा शुक्रिया अदा करती हूं,
कि तूने मेरे लिए इतने अच्छे माता-पिता को चुना है....

21. BERDHISHA

Berdhisha is from Tamil Nadu. She is a poet who
loves to share her own thoughts and imagination.
Furthermore, she loves to write and read novels.
She is a blogger (berdhisha96.), Co-author for about
60+ Anthologies and compiler too. She loves
nature, which is her best friend.

HIS EYES

His eyes are like the brightest star
When I see him,
My mind stays in a kind of war.

His eyes are like volcano,
When he was in anger
But it looks like colorful rainbow.

His eyes are mesmerizing,
It strikes my heart
And allows me to stay in Amnesia.

His eyes are blabbering
Like the magical chants,
It took away my beautiful heart.

His eyes are gleaming
Like Sirius star,
My mind grim to me
Asks me to stay away
But I already forgot myself
By his catty eyes.

22. TAHREEM AFZAL

Tahreem Afzal has done her MS in Mathematics. Besides being a dream hunter, she is the girl who is traveling on the path called 'life'. She doesn't complain for the obstacles, she just makes sure that her faith never gets blurry, as this is the only candle of light which keeps her going in dark nights.

TO THE LOST ONES

While wandering in a garden, I looked at the flowers and got drenched into the ocean of thoughts. They reminded of many souls that left too soon. I asked myself a question: What about those flowers that wilt before their time? It made me sad and hopeless. I felt the pain of those who have lost their dear ones this year. What I would do if I were at their place? I would be broken to pieces like the way they all were broken. But, I want to tell them what I told myself. Apparently, those flowers wilt. Apparently, they disappear from the chapter of life. You will not see them again; you will not feel their presence around. But, does it mean that they are vanished? They don't vanish. They are on the other side. It is for sure that they will greet you when you will reach there. They will accompany you when the right time comes. Till then my dear, keep them alive in your memories.

23. S.SUGANTHI

Suganthi has been writing for over two years. She provides philosophical writings. Her educational background in English literature has given her a broad base for writings. Her books are available in Amazon Kindle named Heartly Sayings and Healing journey-11

HOPE

The hope that has in you
Is like waves of an ocean
It increases and decreases
By the way, you live.
I hope that you have
Some hope on me
I need your waves
In my ocean
With my dreams
Without wings, the bird can't fly.
Without you, my dreams won't fly.
Stay with me until the last
Time of my life.

24. ANKITA MISHRA

I am Ankita Mishra from Cuttack, Odisha. I am a student pursuing my graduation in bachelor's of commerce. Writing was never my passion nor my hobby. All I loved was singing, crafting and playing badminton. Then when I used to stay alone I used to write my feelings no matter happy or sad. And that's how I started writing by expressing my thoughts, feelings and emotions into words. I just hope and look forward towards taking this habit as my passion.

WORK!

No work in this world,
Is small or big
It's your dream,
That you have achieved.

Never compare your work with others,
It's done by your efforts,
All it needs is dedication,
And people as inspiration.

Work is defined by your deeds,
And not by your cheesy talks
Deeds can be good or bad,
Because decision is all yours.

Never take a wrong way,
To make your work grow
Because at the end you'll reap,
That what you have showed.

25. SONAL PRAJAPATI

मैं दिल्ली में रहने वाली सोनल प्रजापति हूं। पेशे से इलेक्ट्रिकल इंजीनियर और जुनून से लेखक। मैं ऑनलाइन लेखन प्रतियोगिता और 80 से अधिक + एंथोलॉजी का हिस्सा रहा हूं। मेरे अधिक उद्धरण, कविताएं, शायरी और कहानियों के लिए मुझे इंस्टाग्राम पर फॉलो करें -मिसराइटर_ मेरे fb अपडेट के लिए कृपया सोनल प्रजापति के विचारों को फॉलो करें

कुछ यादें

बचपन की कुछ यादें यूँ हैं
माँ बाप के इलावा कोई था ही नहीं
दिल में सिर्फ अच्छाई थी
सबके मन में सिर्फ सच्चाई थी
मासूमियत झलका करती थी
एक वो भी दिन थे कमाने की दौड़ ना थी
किसी चीज़ की परवाह ना थी
क्योंकि दुनियादारी की समझ नहीं थी
लेकिन असली जिंदगी हर किसी की वही थी
आँखो में कुछ बड़ा बनने के सपने थे
एक सिर्फ मेरे माँ बाप ही मेरे अपने थे
किसी को दुखी देख कर सोचा करती थी
की मुस्कुरा दे ऐ बंदे जो हो रहा है वही रब की मर्ज़ी थी
मेरे बचपन में बस खुदा से ये मेरी अर्ज़ी थी

26. SRIJA SADHUKHAN

Srija Sadhukhan is 19 years old girl studying B.Sc Biotechnology in Amity University Kolkata. Love to write poetry and a book worm too.

WEIGHING MACHINE

Weighing machines are the most important Object
in our life before anyone else
You weigh our possessions
And the wishes we hold
What about love and care?
If you can't measure these
That our heart itself weaves,
Redundant in weighing machine.
In life always try to balance
What's wrong and what's right?
In weighing balance sometimes
We forget that there is also

Something in between them.

27. RAVISHANKER NISHAD

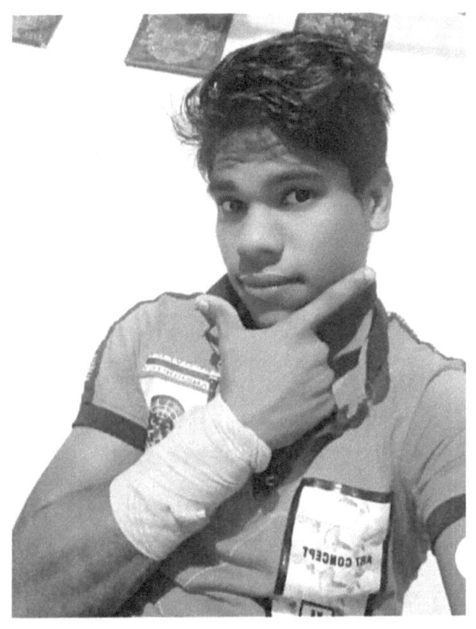

यह रविशंकर निषाद है । ये शाखा:- तमनार, जिला:-
रायगढ़ (छत्तीसगढ़) के निवासी हैं । इनका जन्म 19 जून
2000 में हुआ था ।। यह अभी इंजीनियरिंग कॉलेज में
पढ़ाई कर रहे है । इनकी रुचि कविताएं लिखना है और
यह किताबों के शौकीन भी है ।।

आसूं

दिल के अंदर छुपे भावों को
बहकर कह देते हैं आसूं ।।
चाहे मिले खुशियां सारी
चाहे गमों का सैलाब हो ।।
बिन कहे ही छलक उठते हैं ये मेरे आसूं ।।।
दर्द के समुंदर में तैरते ये मेरे आसूं ।।।
दिल टूट जाता है जब भी
तो निकल पड़ते हैं ये मेरे आसूं ।।
कोई अपना छोड़ जाय
तो टपक पड़ते हैं मेरे आसूं ।।
जिंदगी में ना हो कोई अपना
तो निकल पड़ते हैं ये मेरे आसूं ।।
पिछड़े चाह पर बिछड़े राह पर दोस्त मिल जाय
तो निकल पड़ते हैं मेरे आसूं ।।
तू क्यूं नहीं समझती तेरे बिन
क्यों निकल पड़ते हैं ये मेरे आसूं ।।
मेरे एहसास को मेरे खामोशियां को
बयां कर जाते ये मेरे आसूं ।।

28. PRIYA SINGH

Priya Singh is born & brought up in Dewas,
MadhyaPradesh. She's a proud daughter of her
Father B.N.Singh (T.I.).She's completed Masters of
Computer Science. She is a Former Educationist,
Communication Trainer & Avid Reader.
She's the Co-Author of the Anthologies:-
"It's all about two phase : love & hate" ,"Words
From Heart", "Fierce, Fearless N Flawed" & "In the
way of borehole", "Unseen Blessings & "Sublime
Love", "Mere Papa".
All are available in Amazon.
Till today, she's worked in 200+ Anthologies as a
Co-Author & compiling 3.
Her writing keeps her at ease.
She mostly writes quotes on thoughts.
She loves inspiring young minds.
Instagram id- instant__thoughts_

Let the light of love
Little get deeper as
It shines from within,
It leads us to proximity
Where no one seems akin,
Except the source of light
We are getting as in.
Let it get little high with hopes,
No one could ever imagine it's zest,
It's nothing but a powerful tool
By which not only "You" But also
We can heal.

29. ISHITA SAXENA

She is Ishita Saxena from Bareilly, She has been
Written Since 2Years,
She has been a book co-author 'THE SACRED
SOCIETY'.
She also has written Some her words in a Magazine
by 'THE INKSCRIBBLERS' community.
Even she opened a new writing community named
'ADMIRE OF ILLUSION' herself.

TIME IS ABOUT TO DIE!

Time is about to die!
Who knows when this time will die
Spend your time with those who consider you very
special
Admittedly, time can never come now, but the
movements in them can be kept in memory.
Don't think for the time you lost: now think a little
about yourself and
Who loves you..
This time is very precious, it is not known when
someone gets separated in a moment, but live every
moment so that it does not regret as time passes.
This time is yours. You make a lot of memories in
it, in which some moments are of sadness and
happiness.
Because if you not understand the value of time
That
Time is about to die...

30. AKKSHAYA PRASANNA

Contagious smile, anxious heart, Conscious mind,
gracious me.

TO THE PEOPLE OF YOUNG GENERATION

Run
If you can't run
Walk
If you can't walk
Crawl
But gear up
Education and talents is not the only source for your
future
You define your future
Don't lose hope
Just hop
And go.

31. DAKSHITA JAISWAL

दक्षिता जायसवाल एक 18 वर्षीय प्रबंधन की छात्रा हैं।
वह गोंडा, उत्तरप्रदेश से हैं। एक उत्साही पाठक और
लेखिका होने के नाते उन्होंने कई कार्यक्रम आयोजित
किए हैं और खुद एक कवयित्री, कथाकार, ब्लॉगर और
एक प्रकाशित लेखिका हैं।
वह हैप्पी हार्ट्स संगठन की कोर टीम की सदस्या हैं। वह
लेखन के क्षेत्र में उच्च रुचि रखती हैं और विभिन्न
प्लेटफार्मों पर प्रदर्शन कर चुकी हैं । आप इन्हें इंस्टाग्राम
पर @invoicer_dakshita_jaiswal के नाम से भी खोज
सकते हैं ।

तुझको कविता कहूँ, या खुद को शायरा!

नज़्मों में एक अश्क सा छोड़ा था,
अज्ञात दिशा में यू इश्क़ ने मोड़ा था,
जहाँ ज्ञात सैलाब में एक अज्ञात सा ख्वाब था,
दबी मुस्कुराहटों में उसकी छुअन का एहसास था,
जहाँ उसकी धड़कनों में धड़कते दिल का छिपा राज़ था,
ए ख़ुदा, ये इश्क और मुश्क में जाने कैसा शाज़ था,
जहाँ उसके लबों पर रूहानियत भरा , ऐतबार था,
इख़्तियार में उसकी चुप्पी में छुपा कुछ सार था,
कुछ लम्हों में यून इस क़दर उसमें बसा मेरा संसार था
सही या ग़लत , जाने यह इश्क़ का कैसा वार था,
न दरिया और ना ही दायरा ,
न ज़रिया और ना ही कायरा ,
तुझको कविता कहूँ , या खुद को शायरा!

32. ANKUR MISHRA

बातें अपनी दिल की इस कदर किया करते हैं,
जज़बात को बयां कोरे पन्ने मे किया करते हैं।
ये हैं अंकुर मिश्रा जो वर्तमान मे देवास मध्यप्रदेश मे
कार्यरत एक उभरते हुए लेखक हैं जो कि जिंदगी और
नौकरी का संतुलन बनाये रखते हुए अपने लेखन के शौक
को जिंदा रखे हुए हैं। इनकी रचनाये पच्चीस से ज्यादा ई-
बुक/किताबो मे प्रकाशित हो चुकी या होने वाली हैं।
भविष्य मे ये अपनी सभी रचनाओ को खुद की पुस्तक मे
संजोने का ख्वाब रखते हैं। इंस्टाग्राम मे आप इनसे अपने
विचार ankdip2801 मे साझा कर सकते हैं ।

अपना सफर

थे चल दिये अकेले कोई साथ न था,
किसी भी सहारे का कोई हाथ न था,
कई शक्स थे अक्स पे शक करने को,
तब भी किये जो अधूरे थे सबक करने को,
फलसफे थे बहुत रास्तो के मंजिल पर,
मिला न कोई हमे वो संगदिल मगर,
पशोपेश के झोंके थे वो भी भयंकर,
उलझने बढ़ती ही जा रही थी अंदर,
खत्म न हो रही थी बेचैनी की वो दहक,
सुनाई न दे रही थी उम्मीदो की चहक,
बड़ी लंबी लगने लगी थी उदासी की रातें,
फिर सुनना सबकी खंजर मतलबी बातें,
ऊफ क्यूं नही बसता मजबूत बसेरा,
कब होगा जल्दी से सूकून का सवेरा,
भरोसे की जुबान कम मिली सुनने को,
मशविरा मिला न जब पसंद चुनने को,
हर चीज जिससे हासिल हुआ सिर्फ अश्क,
वो सब छोड़कर किया खुद से ही इश्क।

33. PRAKASH TURIYA

Prakash Turiya from Chhindwara Madhya Pradesh, M.pharma, working as senior executive medical writer.

क्यू आता हैं ये नक्सलवाद।।।।

मन बहुत दुःखता हैं, कलेजा बहुत सुखता हैं।

अक्सर आपदा में, गरीबो का घर ही डूबता हैं।
क्यू नेता, अभिनेता नही होते बर्बाद।
क्यू आता हैं ये नक्सलवाद।।।।

माँ की झोली, पत्नी की मांग को कर सुना।
सरहदों पे बहाते हैं सैनिक खून और पसीना।
छोड़ के चिंता घर की, करते हैं देश को आबाद।
क्यू आता हैं ये नक्सलवाद।।।।

कितना करेंगे सब्र, कितनी खोदेंगे क़ब्र।
कब होंगे हम अपनो से आजाद।
क्यू आता हैं ये नक्सलवाद।।।।
क्यू आता हैं ये नक्सलवाद।।।।

34. PRAKHAR RAGHUWANSHI

I am Prakhar Raghuwanshi from betul city of Madhya Pradesh and I am 15 years old currently studying in class 12th.I have been involved in the field of writing specially in poetry since last one year.

ज़ख्म

कुछ कहा था मैने उसको,

कुछ सुनने को मैं ठहरा था।
शायद कमबख्त ख़यालो का,
उसके दिल पर पहरा था।
जो मैने कहा, लाज़मी नहीं,
ये बोला उसका चेहरा था।
अपना मैं कुछ वापस लिए,
जो एक ख्वाब सुनहरा था।
ग़म की राहो मे भटक गया,
मेरा ज़ख्म ही ज़रा गहरा था।

35. BHAWNA MEHTA

She is presently pursuing B.Ed from Guru
Jambheshwar University, Hisar.She like to pen
down her thoughts. She has written two Blogs and
won Blog Competition also.

सच से रूबरू

क्यो बहस करू किसी से,
जब मेरे अपने ही गैर बने,
याद हैं अब मुझे किसने किस वक्त पर,
पीठ पर वार करे,
बेशक बोले नहीं किसी को कुछ,
सब जन कर भी,
अंजान बने रहे,
सब कुछ चुप चाप सी सहते रहे,
मगर जबान क्या करें जब मेरे अपने ही आस्तीन के सांप
निकले

36. MANSI SOLANKI

Mansi Solanki from Navsari, Gujarat. She is currently pursing diploma civil engineering from Uka Tarsadia University. She have started writing a month ago and she loves to write poems, shayari, quotes, one-liner. She is Co-Author of 40+ anthologies and thank you for giving her chance for this anthology.

QUOTES

1) His scent was her addiction, like she loved his fragrance on her clothes and that makes her feel his presence real around her.

2) Love is not a gift it is a beautiful feeling which need oceans of ink to describe in best sense.

3) In your arms my paradise lies,
I wanna fly like a bird in your skies.
Charms of your smile make me feel your deepest desires,
Rest of your love and care inspires.

37. NAVEEN BHARDWAJ

He is Naveen Bhardwaj a programmer by
profession a lover of poetry maker and like reading
books and audiobooks and he has telegram channel
@TheNBbook

Insta I'd na.vin7832

LIFE DECISION

There is no good and bad decisions in life only lesson learn if you think you made bad and spontaneous decision then it will be bad decision only. But if you think the decision taken by you are good for you it will give you result in future extend.

One percent growth everyday is better than no growth. Keeps taking small and gradual action every day which brings you closer to your goals. Rather sitting idle and doing nothing. Always remember growth maybe is minor but the outcome will be undesirable.

Sometimes life doesn't give you what you want it doesn't mean you don't deserve it. It means life wants to give you more. So stop blaming to anyone for your failure take responsibility, and move onto next mission.

38. ANUSHA SATHIA

Anusha is a writer and a poet hailing from India. She is currently in high school. She has been writing since quite a few years and that has been her passion. She uses her positive attitude and tireless energy to encourage others to work hard and succeed and she writes because she enjoys expressing herself. For more of her work, please check out her Instagram handle: @_thelittletherapist

ALL THESE BLANK PAGES ARE WAITING FOR ME

To stain them with the emotions I've rarely shown

To give shape to all the thoughts I've borne
To fold my dreams in planes and let them fly
To drench them in my tears till they have run dry
To unravel my deepest desires between their lines
To bury the name of my crush under a million heart
signs
To scribble doodles in their corners when I'm bored
To pen poetries about the people I adored
To draw on them maps to the places I want to go
To spill the secrets that the others will never know

These blank pages wait for me to make them my
friend
To start filling them up with life and to never end.

39. N. KRISHNAVENI

N. Krishnaveni is an aspiring writer and a budding poet. One of her poems "My Beloved Damsel!" has published in The Literary Herald journal. She is a co-author of many anthologies. She won the Spectrum Budding Writer Award 2021. Most of her poems deal with the theme of nature, human emotions, and philosophical thoughts. Her poetry voices out the deepest emotions and secrets that are left unspoken and destined to be beautifully inked. Having a creative artistic propaganda, her writings hail from the articulate thoughts with coherence, spontaneity and flowery language.

ECLIPSE

The incessant chirping of the birds
Marks the beginning of the day
Souls stuck between the tornado of chaos
And the beautiful dawn with new hope.
Rummaging every nooks in the Earth
To find a safer place than this.
Fantasizing by the reverie that is precise
Exhausted eyes falls asleep
And intrigued in the dream of island.
Two celestial spheres meet in a line
Partially darks the right face
Often we lament the dark night
But recklessly ignores the bright destiny ahead.
Motherly birdie tend to shield her squab heir
From the wordly darkness noxiously outspread.

40. DEESHA SONI

Deesha Soni, a Post Graduate and M.phil adorns the hat of a multitasker of an educationist, artist, poet, photographer, author, blogger, homemaker, wife and mother. She has 10 years experience in the field of Education as a Professor and Coordinator.Deesha has various publications to her credit in national and international levels. Deesha has various published works to her credit... she has two books published on Amazon... named 'Just thoughts' and 'Random thoughts on pandemic'...Kindle edition and more than 100 plus published works on various online platforms of.. Deesha has been twice nominated for Author of a week award by Story mirror and has also won various recognitions in penning stories and write-ups.. at National and International levels. Deesha has various published works to her credit... she has two books published on Amazon... named 'Just thoughts' and 'Random thoughts on pandemic'..Kindle edition has also won many prizes in National and international levels in many write-ups. Deesha has also published her works in 300 plus anthologies of multiple genres...

THE LOST TREASURE

The lost treasure...

Lost is a precious treasure...
In life's tremendous pressure..
The pleasures of living we've forgot...
In deadlines.... earnings.... prolonged working...
we're caught...
Flavours of life aren't relished anymore...
Insecurities... Competition...is left in store...
It's beyond understanding... are we running a
Marathon???
The little pleasures we cherished are somewhere
gone....
The ultimate treasure is living with peace and
satisfaction...
Yet materialism...and false showoffs is centre of
attraction...
Sit back...Feel the breeze.... thinks for a while...
The soothing moon... fresh grass dews.... are bound
to bring a smile...
For god sake....Lift your head...from your mobile
handset...
Play with your lil one... It's monsoon time...do get
wet...
Work shall never get over...It's infinite and
perpetual...
Money and Riches...are just not the goals ...gain bit
by bit.... life's lost treasure...

41. YOGESH GURJAR CHINU

इनका नाम योगेश गुर्जर है और निकनेम चीनू है, यह उत्तरप्रदेश के गौतम बुद्ध नगर जिले से है।

इन्हें थॉट्स लिखना और पढ़ना बहुत पसंद है, पोएट्री और कोट्स 1300 से ज्यादा लिख चुकी है।
420 Anthology में Co-author के रूप में लिख चुकी है। इनकी पहली सोलो बुक जिसका नाम (सच्ची बातें "चीनू") है।

बारिश का आनंद

कड़ी धूप में बे-मौसम बारिश होते देखा,

बादलों को जब मैंने आता देखा,

मन में बस एक ही ख्याल आया,
बेसन ले जाने का ध्यान आया,

पता है क्या है बारिश की असली पहचान,
चाय और पकौड़े से स्वागत करता है इंसान,

दोस्तों को चाय पे घर बुलाया,
चाय-पकौड़े से उनका स्वाद बनाया,

बरसात में सभी को पसंद आता है भुट्टा,
मज़ा तो तब है जब सभी खाये होके इकट्ठा,

फिर दोस्तों संग एक प्रोग्राम बनाया,
बारिश में नहाते हुए ठेले पर भुट्टा खाया,

इस बारिश को हमनें यादगार बनाया,
जीवन के कुछ पल को हमनें आनन्दमय बनाया....!!

42. POETRY KHAKHOLIA

नमस्कार, ये है पोइट्री खाखोलिया
गुवाहाटी असम से, बीयालिस वर्ष, कॉन्वेंट एजुकेटेड ,
शादीशुदा दो बच्चे है। इन्होंने एमकॉम,
म.इड, एलएलबी किया है पर लिखना इनकी रुचि रही है
स्कूल से ही और अब इसी क्षेत्र में एक मुकाम अर्जित
करना चाहती। इन्होंने चालीस से ज्यादा अंथोलॉजी में
अपनी लेखनी से नवाजा है और कहानी किताब भी लिख
रही है जो जल्द ही आने वाली। लिखना सिर्फ काम नहीं
बल्कि जुनून है इनके लिए जो ये हर पल जीती।
आशा है आप सभी को इनकी रचना पसंद आए।

प्रेरक उद्धरण

1. तुम्हारे लिए मेरा प्यार
पानी से भरा ग्लास है
जो मुझे आधा भरा दिखता और
भरने की गुंजाइश होती वहीं तुम्हे आधा खाली नजर आता
और वो भी खत्म होता दिखता

2. रंजिश में अक्सर
हम खुद को मिटा देते
खुद को ही भुला देते
भला किसी का होता नहीं
हां नुकसान जरूर होता
खुद के सिवाय किसी ओर का कुछ नहीं बिगड़ता

3. मोहब्बत इतनी है कि अब तेरे सिवा कुछ नहीं भाता
कुछ नहीं चाहता एक तेरी चाहत के सीवा
बस तेरी बाहों में जी लगता एक
उम्र गुज़ार दु तेरी पनाह में ऐसा लगता

43. KAJAL BHARGAV

काजल भार्गव यह लखनऊ से है इन्हे लिखना, पढ़ना, घूमना पसंद है यह भविष्य में लेखक और अध्यापक बनना चाहती है इनका सपना अनाथ आश्रम बनाने का है।

एक दिन.....

दिन एक एक करके ता उम्र गुजार देते है
हम किसी के,कोई हमारा यही भ्रम पालते है।

बिना मेहनत, सब पाने की कोशिश करते है
भाग्य भरोसे बैठकर तकदीर को कोश्ते है।

प्रेम भाव रखकर भी हम क्रोध में जलते है
चार दिन की जिंदगी में कितनी ईर्ष्या पालते है।

मैने एक शाम बारिश में भीगकर देखा है
जन्नत तो नही पर जन्नत सी खुशी मिलती है।

जिंदगी को हंसकर गले से लगा लेती हूं
अब किसी के लिए टूट कर नही बिखरती हूं ।

तुम्हे कोई आगे बढ़ने की सलाह देता है
तो तुम आगे बढ़ना पर सीखते सीखते।

जीवन के कुछ रिश्ते कच्चे धागे से होते है
जरा सा खींचते ही वह पूरी तरह टूटते है ।

खुद को मजबूत बनाना हो तो आग में तपना
फिर तुम टूट तो सकोगे पर बिखर नही सकते ।

44. ANAMIKA

अनामिका, जो एक कला शिक्षक हैं , मुरादाबाद, उत्तर प्रदेश की रहने वाली हैं । इन्हे अपने विचारों और अनुभवों को काव्यात्मक तरीके से लिखना पसंद है। जो इन्हें शांति और संतुष्टि देता है। किसी ऐसे व्यक्ति से बात कर रही हैं, जो इनके विचारों पर पूर्वाग्रह या निर्णय नहीं ले रहा है । अनामिका ने अपनी भावनाओं ,अपनी सोच और अपने विचारों को कविताओं के माध्यम से व्यक्त करने की कोशिश की है। यह इस से पहले 80+ पद्यावली में अपनी रचनाएँ संकलित कर चुकी हैं,आशा है आप सब इसे पसंद करेंगे।

ज़रूरी है??

आज का दौर नया है,
सीखने को बहुत कुछ नया है,
बदलाव हर क्षेत्र में ज़रूरी है,
सहूलियत की ख़ातिर लैपटॉप कंप्यूटर ज़रूरी है,
तो शादी ब्याह में फालतू खर्चा क्यों ज़रूरी है,
व्यापार के लिए सही ताल मेल ज़रूरी है,
तो शादी ब्याह में गाय भैंस की तरह
किसी भी खूँटे से बाँधना क्या मज़बूरी है?
बदलते दौर के साथ बदलना ज़रूरी है,
कुछ बड़े समझें कुछ छोटे...
बीच का रास्ता निकालना ज़रूरी है ,
आज के दौर में भी
लड़कियों के लिए "पराया धन" शब्द कहाँ ज़रूरी है?
लड़को के सामान उन्हें भी
ज़िन्दगी जीने का हक़ देना ज़रूरी है....
कुछ सपने उनके भी संजोना ज़रूरी है,
हर ज़िन्दगी का मुक़ाम शादी पर मुकम्मल हो
यह ज़रूरी नहीं,
कुछ उनके भी लक्ष्य हैं यह जानना ज़रूरी है
शादी की कहाँ कोई उम्र होती है,
पर सपने तोड़ने के लिए वह खुद में सम्पूर्ण होती है...

45. MS. ISHRAT JAHAN NOORMOHAMMED KHAN

Ms Ishrat jahan khan is a passionate Teacher and a Writer she loves reading and writing. Loving and caring is her hobby. And keep learning and accept the positive suggestion is her quality.
She belongs to North India and stays at Ulhasnagar (Maharashtra).
Loves humanity always.

YOUNG FELLOWS

Young fellows
Few of them like yellows
Few are mellow
And few are just fellow

Life makes magic
With the tragic
And we become sad
With lot of lad

Fine is a word to say
Or else life always pays
And it keeps on toe
And sometime low

Young fellows
Few of them like yellows
Few are mellow
And few are just fellow

46. SRAVANI KOMMAYYA

"Believe in what you do.!"

Here Herself Sravani Kommayya who is known as Srk.She believes that writing and exploring are not only hobbies, but also the building blocks of perfect thinking. She is an enthusiastic and pleasant learner and ofcourse writing passionate. She is in process of becoming her father's pride...
IG - @voice.of_her

WILL THEY STAY FOREVER?

Your heart is not
A store room
To keep
All their unwanted things
Clear all the zunk
Then just chill.

Still are you thinking about them?
If your answer is yes!
Then lemme know what's the use of it?
Are they will comeback? Yes maybe!
Then can you love Them Again.? Yes maybe
Will they stay forever? No Way...
So it's better to Stop everything and Just chill...

47. MIHIR PATHAK

Mihir Pathak is a good writer from Jamnagar Gujrat. He has completed his 12th in commerce stream. He has been writing stories for 2 years as his passion. He wants to be a film writer in future.

प्यार Vs दोस्ती

एक रोहन नाम का लड़का और अनुषा नाम की लड़की दोनों बचपन से खास दोस्त है। रोहन अनुषा को बचपन से प्यार करता था, लेकिन दोस्ती टूटने की वजह से बता नहीं पा रहा था। तो दूसरी तरफ अनुषा किसी राहुल नाम के लड़के के साथ रिलेशनशिप में थी पर राहुल के चीट करने की वजह से अनुषा ने उसके साथ ब्रेकअप कर लिया। और एक दिन कार्तिक यानी रोहन के दोस्त ने रोहन को अपने प्यार के बारे में अनुषा को बताने की हिम्मत देता है और फिर रोहन अनुषा को पार्क में बुलाता है। और फिर रोहन अनुषा को बोलता है , " मैं तुमसे प्यार करता हूं। अनुषा विल यू बी माय गर्लफ्रेंड " और अनुषा कहती है " देखो रोहन तुम मेरे सबसे अच्छे दोस्त हो और मैं भी तुमसे प्यार करती हूं पर तुमसे यह आशिकी नहीं , क्योंकि तू मेरी ताकत है, मेरी कमजोरी नहीं और राहुल मेरी कमजोरी था। और फिर दो-तीन दिन बाद दोनों फिर से अच्छे दोस्त की तरह रहने लगे और रोहन ने समझ लिया कि प्यार करने के लिए गर्लफ्रेंड की जरूर नहीं।

48. YUVASRI YELLETI

Hello there...She is YuvaSri...a writer by her own
Choice...she loves to write and trying to spread her
wings through her writings!

ACCEPTANCE - PROGRESS

"The acceptance you offer yourself...
Shouldn't be a barrier for your progress!"

.

Now-a-days the most common phrases that we are
listening are "Accept yourself", "Accept the way
you are"...
When coming to my conscience, the phrase should
be continued as "Accept yourself...and shine the
way you are"...
Yes it's important to offer the acceptance to ourself
and always keep in your mind
That it shouldn't neither be a barrier nor spoiler.
Remember.,
Progress is seen only where the change initiates...
Change can be of various...in thoughts...in acts...lot
and more...
So,
Accept the way you are...
And shine the way you are!

49. NEERAJ. J

Neeraj was born on 23rd December 2000 in Chennai. He is good at solving mathematical problems which relates to life situations and he is also a good writer and compiled around 30 anthologies so far. To succeed he always follow this " Enjoy the goodness and the badness of the life always".

THE RELIEVED ONE

One who gets it
Will survive till for last
Those who had made it
Will give it so fast
Relief is not a game
It's a life pain
Which wont be same
For everyone who claim
The one who relieve
Will succeed
And no one bares
Who get those scares
Will once succumb
That makes everyone to tear
Their own share
Which everyone dont

Will wait for those fonts.

50. SMITA NAIDU

Smita Naidu is a computer post graduate with double diploma, MCA, DCA, DISM, CPISM, this is her qualification, she is working as a business head of procode technologies, which is an IT company, she is also a writer, translator, transcriber, graphic designer, entrepreneur, Youtuber, recruiter, life coach and a podcaster. As a writer, she has published more than 500. Plus quotes, which are visible on Google too, she has published a few books as coauthor too, and several are piled up, her solo book will also be published soon! She was also into forever book of world record recently, as an emerging entrepreneur.

TODAY'S YOUTH

They are energetic, but they sadly dont know to
boost it into others;

They need respect, but they sadly dont know to give
it to others;

They need love, but they sadly dont know how to
shower it to others;

They need enjoyment, but they sadly dont know
how to rejoice for what reasons, and with whom or
in what way;

They are smart, but they sadly dont understand the
hazards of being over smart;

They need quick success, but they sadly don't know
the importance of hard and smart work and also
perseverance;

They need time to take decisions, but just cant have
any patience;

Oh dear youngsters, please understand and apply all
the life virtues, and then you will surely be
unstoppable!